"Our Art Deco is worth preserving because it connects Tulsa to a fascinating time in its history - an era of oil-boom wealth."

William Franklin

Tulsa Art Deco Top10

To Mary Ellen Strakoulas, my inspiration, support and the one I truly love.

Don Wagner

Published by :

Oklahoma Tourist Guides Inc.
www.Tulsa-Books.com
(918) 693-1198
DON.WAGNER.OK@GMAIL.COM

Edited By Mary Ellen Strakoulas

A special thanks goes to
        Seed Technologies Inc. for the Cover Design
        Jennifer Jones (918) 742-0028
        Graphic Artist: Tony Lyons

ISBN 978-1-4276-3940-0
51999

9 781427 639400

1

TABLE OF CONTENTS

When I published "Tulsa Art Deco Experience", I tried to provide a comprehensive visual guide to the Art Deco architecture in Tulsa. Due to space constraints and the overwhelming number of deco buildings in Tulsa, I was unable to display the fine detail and craftsmanship that makes these structures so special. They are more than just buildings, they are pieces of art. This book focuses on Tulsa's top ten Art Deco buildings and shows more detail of those 10 buildings.

Most of the Tulsa Art Deco is of the Zigzag style that emphasizes strong vertical lines and geometric patterns. This includes Boston Ave. Methodist Church, Farmers Market, Oklahoma Natural Gas and the Philcade building.

The PWA/Depression style of architecture was funded partially with public money in a period that included recovery from the Great Depression. The Fair Grounds Pavilion, Tulsa Union Depot, Daniel Webster High School and Will Rogers High School are examples of this style.

The Streamline style is more horizontally oriented and typically features aerodynamic flowing curves. Examples of this style are The Brook Restaurant, City Veterinary and Day & Nite Cleaners.

See a comprehensive list of Art Deco in our previous book. "Tulsa Art Deco Experience".

TULSA DECO DISTRICT

The Deco District in the central part of downtown Tulsa was formed to promote downtown business enterprise by highlighting the rich Art Deco architecture and history. The district is located from 1st to 8th street and from Cincinnati to Denver Avenue. This unofficial boundary has one of the most concentrated collections of Art Deco architecture in the country. This includes Central High School, SW Bell Main Dial Building, Tulsa Club, Day Building, Mayo Motor Inn, Service Pipeline Building and Public Service Co. Building. Also in this district are the Philcade Building, Gillette-Tyrell Building and Oklahoma Natural Gas Building which are covered in detail.

Central High School

Day Building

Public Service Co. Building

Mayo Motor Inn

Service Pipeline Building

SW Bell Main Dial Building

The designation of the Tulsa Deco District has generated additional interest in the architecture downtown. Maps of self guided walking tours are available from the from the Tulsa Historical Society and the Decopolis Gallery.

Decopolis Studios, an Art Deco centric store, at 607 South Boston provides a variety of deco inspired furniture and accessories. Store owner William Franklin and Dr. Christopher McDaniels are premier promoters of Tulsa Art Deco. They are founders of the Annual Deco Ball, Art Deco Museum and window displays at the Philcade.

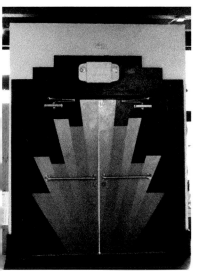

DEFINITION OF TERMS

Through the book we use terms unfamiliar to the general public. Some of those terms are defined for better understanding.

Apron - a raised section of ornamental stonework below a window ledge or roof line, typically stone tablet, or monument.

Chevron - a zigzag molding shaped like an upside down V.

Buttress - an architectural structure built against or projecting from a wall which serves to support or reinforce the wall.

Cantilever - an unsupported overhang acting as a lever, like a flagpole sticking out of the side of a wall.

Cornice - upper section of an entablature, a projecting shelf along the top of a wall often supported by brackets.

Crocket - a hook-shaped decorative element common in Gothic architecture.

Dormer - a structural element of a building that protrudes from the plane of a sloping roof.

Façade - a visible surface like the face of a building.

Finials - an architectural decorative device used at the top, end, or corner of a structure.

Foyer - an entrance hall or other open area in a building.

Gable - the generally triangular portion of a wall between the edges of a sloping roof.

Inset - something smaller inserted into some larger thing.

Parapet - a low wall projecting from the edge of a platform, terrace, or roof.

Latticework - a framework consisting of a criss-crossed pattern of strips of building material.

Molding - a strip of material with various profiles used to cover transitions between surfaces or for decoration.

Pilaster - a slightly projecting column built into or applied to the face of a wall.

Portico - a porch leading to the entrance of a building.

Shard - a sharp broken piece of glass or metal.

Spandrel - the space between two arches or between an arch and a rectangular enclosure.

Terra-cotta - fired clay used especially for statuettes and other architectural design purposes.

Vestibule - a lobby, entrance hall, or passage between the entrance and the interior of a building.

HOW TOP 10 WAS CALCULATED

The top 10 was calculated by empirically calculating a subjective evaluation of each of the most significant Art Deco sites in Tulsa. Each site was evaluated on its Exterior, Interior and Extra Features.

Exterior Features

- Strong linear impression
- Geometric ornamentation
- Decorative panels and facades
- Windows with decorative spandels
- Reeds and fluting around doors and windows
- Zigzags, chevrons

Interior Features

- Complex groupings of geometric shapes
- Bands of color
- Zigzag designs
- Cubic forms
- Stylized decorative interiors
- Smooth wall surfaces

Extra Features

The Extra Features are special items unique to the interior or exterior of the structure, for example the Art Deco museum in the Philcade building or the huge mural in the auditorium at Will Rogers High School.

After evaluating each building, a score between 0 and 4 was assigned for each category (Exterior, Interior, Special) at each art deco site. A category weight factor was applied to each category and a total score was calculated for each building. The buildings were then ranked by that score. If you want a copy of the evaluation tables, email your request to:

Don.Wagner.OK@Gmail.Com

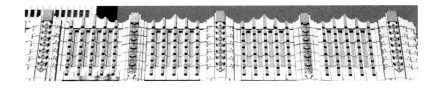

TULSA ART DECO TOP 10

1. Boston Avenue Methodist Church
2. Philcade Building
3. Will Rogers High School
4. Gillette Tyrrell Building
5. Christ the King Parish
6. Union Depot
7. Oklahoma Natural Gas
8. Fire Alarm Building
9. Fairgrounds Pavilion
10. Warehouse / Farmers

HONORABLE MENTION:

Richard Lloyd Jones Residence (Westhope)
Daniel Webster High School
Riverside Studio

DISCLAIMER

The buildings selected in Tulsa Art Deco Top 10 reflect the opinions of Don Wagner and are in no way an endorsement of one building over another and are in no way intended to slight or diminish the beauty and value of any building or houses not in this list.

OKLAHOMA TOURIST GUIDES

Boston Avenue Methodist Church, is a landmark with significant national reputation as one of the world's top Art Deco Masterpieces. It was the first church in the country designed in a strictly American style of architecture.

The church design was the collaboration of Adah Robinson, a Tulsa Central High School art teacher, and a former student, architect Bruce Goff. Robinson studied the history and traditions of the Methodist faith for a year in advance of developing the church design. Her initial design sketches expanded by Goff into structural plans.

The church has a 250 foot center with west and east wing attachments. On the east side is the Education Wing and on the west side is the semi-circle shaped sanctuary. The building is listed on the National Register of Historic Places (1978) and is Tulsa's only National Historic Landmark (1999). The Church is a Zigzag Art Deco style with strong vertical accents.

THE TOWER
The most dominant feature of the church's exterior is the 15 storied tower that houses office space. Straight, vertical lines are emphasized by concrete columns. This design suggests the church's reaching up to God.

All religious interpretations for this section of the book comes from the website of the Boston Avenue Methodist Church.

EXTERIOR DESIGN

LANTERNS

Art Deco styled lanterns light the property boundaries, steps and entry ways to the church.

HANDS IN PRAYER

At the top of the tower, are finials representing hands raised upward in prayer.
Sixty – six pairs of praying hands are found in the ornamentation around the church exterior. The hands are open in prayer signifying the openness to receive God's blessing. At the top of the tower, is a steel and glass enclosure of window panes in a chevron pattern.

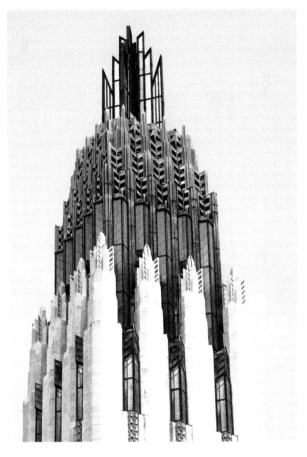

Built: 1929
Deco Style: Zigzag
Architect: Bruce Goff
Rush, Endicott & Rush
Artist: Adah Robinson
Robert Garrison
NRIS: 78002270
Address: 1301 S. Boston Ave.

Above both the north and south doors are terra-cotta statues created by sculptor, Robert Garrison, a former student of Adah Robinson.

The south face of the building displays The Methodist Circuit Riders and a series of Worshipers in Prayer.

THE CIRCUIT RIDERS

The "Circuit Riders" over the south doors are the representations of early Methodist evangelists spreading the word of God by horse back through Europe and America. The statue figures on each end represent two prominent early American Methodist ministers, Bishop William McKendrie, and Bishop Francis Asbury (America's first Methodist Bishop). The rider in the center is symbolic of all the others who spread God's word and is represented by a depiction of Reverend T.L. Darnell, an early American circuit rider, who was the father-in-Law of the church minister.

WORSHIPERS IN PRAYER

Above the north and south sanctuary doors are three groups of people with their hands together in prayer. These statues represent the three aspects of Spiritual life (Religious, Education and Worship).

Three angled arched doorways are covered by the "Worshipers in Prayer" statues. The architectural elements such as the doors, porticos and pilasters emphasize a vertical ascent to the heavens. This implies a connection with God as the tower transcends to the heavens.

THE WESLEY'S

Above the north doors to the church sanctuary are two sets of terracotta figures of historical significance to Methodists. Above the triangular arched doors are the Portrait Sculptures of the Wesley's. In the center is John Wesley, founder of the Methodist Church. His mother, Susana is to the left and to the right is his brother, Charles who wrote over 1000 Methodist hymns. The triangular elements in the columns suggest a blessing from God to all who enter these doors.

WEST FACE

The west end of the building houses the sanctuary. It is encircled by stained glass windows, with terracotta pinnacles, sandwiched between concrete buttresses.

GOD'S LIGHT

The golden terracotta with flowing downward lines represents the outpouring of God's love, a theme that is echoed in the stained glass and interior of the church.

SEVEN POINT STARS

Seven pointed stars used throughout the church represent the seven virtues of man. (faith, hope, charity, fortitude, justice, temperance, and prudence).

CHILDREN'S BUILDING

East of the original building is a new annex called the Children's Building". It was built to match the decor and the art deco architecture of the original building.

Notice the angular shape of the windows and doors.

Built: 2002
Deco Style: Zigzag
Architect: Roger Coffee
Artist: Richard Bohm
              Phyllis Mantik

INTERIOR DESIGN

COLUMBARIUM

Located in the "Children's Building", just off the main entry hall, the columbarium is a burial place for members selecting cremation as a burial choice.

As you enter the doors, you pass a marble statue of a woman in prayer. On either side are large brass engravings depicting the shared mourning of God with humans. The stained glass windows and doors were designed and created by Tulsan, Richard Bohm. Above the columbarium a 10-foot-wide skylight provides a view of the church tower.

GREAT HALL

On the east side of the sanctuary is a long hallway called the "Great Hall". It has high walls with a series of pilasters topped by triangular arches. Between these units are skylights above and deco styled lanterns along the walls to decorate and light the hall. The hall is said to have exceptional acoustics.

The shade of pink, used throughout the church, is highly accentuated by this long hall.

At each end of the Great Hall hang large mosaics designed by Chicago artist, Angelo Gheradi in 1993 to celebrate the church's 100th anniversary. Each mosaic is constructed of about 250,000 venetian tiles and weights over 3000 pounds.

The theme of the two murals is how God was revealed to us in both the Old Testament and New Testament scriptures.

The North Mosaic represents the Hebrew scriptures and depicts the Torah Scroll, the prophet staff and the burning bush. At the top of the mosaic is the representation that from nothing God created everything.

The South Mosaic represents the Christian scriptures depicting the cave where Christ was born, the sacraments of the Protestant faith and crucifixion cross. The radiating triangles represent the power of the trinity.

Sanctuary

The Sanctuary is a combination of all the Adah Robinson artistic themes represented in an art deco style. The entrances are through doors on the north and south. The west side is semicircular and holds tall, narrow, leaded, stained glass windows. On the east side is a rectangular area containing the organ and choir stalls. The seating is located in center of the room, which is divided into five triangular sections of pews and aisles leading to the altar. The orientation of the aisles along with wall pilasters focuses one's attention to the altar. Finely carved woodwork includes tall, narrow, chevron-like tritoma spears adorning the choir stalls, heater vents, altar and screen. beneath the cross.

Behind the altar is a huge 750,000-piece mosaic glass mural.

The seats and benches around the altar are upholstered with art deco designed cushions.

Decorative organ pipes are located on each side of the tabernacle mirroring the design of the doorway arches.

STAINED GLASS WINDOWS

Light is a major symbol emphasized in the design throughout the church. Eleven black-metal framed colored stained glass windows encircle the west end of the sanctuary.

Each window is configured in a "W" like configuration to project maximum light regardless of the sun's position. The downward-flowing lines in the window design symbolize the outpouring of God's love.

Two flowers indigenous to Oklahoma are displayed in the window design to signify vital, growing Christianity.

The coreopsis, which grows in the driest soil, symbolizes the hardiness and joy of the Christian faith.

The tritoma, or torch lily, with its unusual downward blossoms, represents the generosity of the faith. Its strong stem is indicative of the strength of the church.

Sanctuary Dome

The ceiling is domed, with a massive circular elaboration of chevrons radiating from the center. A leaded-glass skylight is in the center of the dome. The dome was designed to symbolize the infinite nature of God hovering over the congregation below.

2. THE PHILCADE BUILDING

A beautiful Art Deco interior is in the Philcade Building at 511 South Boston.

It is a zigzag styled design with strong exterior definition and an absolutely beautiful interior displaying multiple art deco features.

The building's east-west lobby hallway has five painted Art Deco ceiling murals.

At the east end of lobby is the Tulsa Art Deco Museum. The museum displays deco artifacts and sells deco books, art and other deco items.

Window displays of various art deco objects are displayed through the north-south lobby hallway.

The lobby has Deco Styled Elevators. All these features have made the Philcade one of Tulsa's top art deco buildings.

Built:	1930
Deco Style:	Zigzag
Architects:	Smith & Senter
Artist	Channing Stewart
NRIS:	86002196
Address:	

EXTERIOR DESIGN

The Philcade is a thirteen story building located on the southeast corner of Boston Avenue and Fifth Street. It is a Zigzag Art Deco styled building with strong vertical features emphasized by vertical chevrons on the side of the building that extend from the second floor to the roof. The exterior is brick matching the Philtower Building across the street. The doors of the of the two buildings are aligned to provide harmony between the two buildings.

The structure is actually three inter connected buildings with a shared lobby. The first two floors of the building were constructed as commercial store fronts with exterior display windows framed by a series of terracotta patterns.

The first and second floor are covered with carved terra cotta and cast iron veneer. Between the floors are a series of decorative chevrons shown in the picture on the left. The building entrance has a pair of doors covered by an inset portico. Decorative deco patterns frame the glass above the doors.

The roof line features terracotta trim on the north face of the building and is shown below. Notice the staggered pyramid finials capping the vertical chevrons that run the length of the building. The roof has an apron with repeating patterns topped by cut outs exposing the sky.

The roof line of the west face of the building is shown above. It has a different appearance than the north face of the building. It terminates the vertical chevrons with a different pyramid and has a simpler apron pattern.

INTERIOR DESIGN

ENTRY WAY

Above the north portico doors is a gold leaf design and decorative air vent that with the marble vertical walls frames the art deco designed windows above the doors.

The Philcade lobby features polished St. Genevieve marble walls and arches forming a ceiling covered in gold leaf ornamental plaster and hand painted Zigzag Art Deco geometric designs. The arches are connected to the floor by lavish marble pilasters.

The hallway is lit by a series of deco styled brass and glass chandeliers centered in an octagon within a square.

The coordinated color scheme of the interior is muted tones of red, blue, green, purple, and brown, popular art deco colors of the 1920-1930 time period.

Along the north-south foyer are a series of mahogany framed store display windows. These provided a 1920's version of modern shopping malls. Today most of these windows display examples of art deco designed items. They are available for viewing whenever the building lobby is open.

Windows include displays of:
- Apparel & Accessories
- Appliances & Household Items
- China
- Decorations
- Ash trays
- Artwork, Statues & Pictures

These displays along with the museum gift store -visitor center comprise the Art Deco Museum that is staffed and maintained by volunteers.

The Philcade lobby was built in the shape of a "T" for Tulsa. The east-west hall forms the top of the "T". The tan and black terrazzo floors exhibit large deco square blocks. At the intersection of the major hallways are a series of elevators with an interior deco design.

At the east end of the east-west foyer is the Art Deco Museum's Gift Shop and Visitor Center. The lobby window displays, gift shop and visitor center comprise the "Tulsa Art Deco Museum", an ongoing development project cultivated by artist William Franklin, proprietor of the Decopolis Studio.

It is funded by donations, gift shop profits and the annual fundraiser, "The Deco Ball". Information about the museum's activities can be found at:

www.TulsaArtDecoMuseum.com

The gift shop – visitor center is operated by volunteers. The museum utilizes the interior showcase windows to display its art deco exhibits within a great Art Deco. It enhances the tourism potential of the Tulsa Deco District and generates local interest in a Tulsa treasure.

A special thanks to William Franklin,
Dr. Chris McDaniels, Charla and Mike Lowry, Debbie Kelsey, Jennifer Butler and John Eakins without whose efforts this unique museum would not exist.

The east-west foyer is lit by chandeliers centered within deco designed Zigzag Art Deco murals typical of that era. Where the north-south hall repeats a deco design, the east-west hall displays a distinct mural for each chandelier. The murals were designed and painted by local artist Channing Stewart.

Will Rogers High School was built and opened in 1938. Designed by Leon B. Senter and Joseph R. Koberling, Jr., it is of the PWA style of Art Deco architecture, with a great deal of craftsmanship artistry throughout the building.   Shortly after opening Rogers High School was featured in a Time Magazine article "outlining the high school pattern of the future". The school was called "a model progressive high school" in "one of the most progressive school systems in the study."

Today Will Rogers College High School occupies the building. Students attend from grades 6 through 12 and can graduate with a College Associates Degree.

The goal of the architects was to create a friendly and inviting environment reminiscent of Will Roger's personality. They carefully designed 101 architectural and artistic features to realize this goal. They beautifully integrated the modern architecture of the day with quality materials and good craftsmanship.

Built: 1938
Deco Style: PWA
Designed By: Leon B. Senter & Joseph R.
Artist: Alex C. Rindskoph
Joseph R. Koberling
NRIS: 07000918
Address: 3909 E. 5th Place

TOWERS
The elaborate buff brick school features two large towers at the front entry way to the building.   Each encases a stairwell that connects four floors of classrooms. Alternating sections of terra cotta and windows provide natural light in the stairways. The towers are supported by stepped pilasters with ornate details in terra cotta capitals.

VESTIBULE DOORS
Art Deco doors covered by a terra cotta panels are painted a contrasting pale green.

WILL ROGERS PANELS
Two tetra cotta panels above the west doors feature Will Roger's life in two phases. One depicts his cowboy days with a horse, roped steer, and the prairie, and the other his movie days with a reel camera, airplane, and polo rider.

East Exterior Entry

Lanterns

Lighting each entry is a pair of art deco lanterns. The door on the west end of the school has sconces whereas the east entryway has free standing lanterns.

Education Panels

The two terra cotta sculptures above the eastern doors are of a boy and girl student with educational themed items. The plaques were designed by architect Joseph R. Koberling.

WEST INTERIOR

The west entryway is the most impressive with wide steps leading to the foyer covered by terrazzo floors in an art deco pattern. On either side of foyer are impressively wide stairs connecting the upper floors of the building through the tower.

The alcove at the back of the picture leads to the stairwell for the first floor of the building. You actually enter the building on the second floor. Most enclaves and doorways are decorated with gold trimmed tile panels.

The Bust of Will Rogers is popular with students who rub his head when passing for good luck.

38

MAIN HALL

The main hallway, connecting the east and west doors, is lit by decorative hanging lamps. There are several commemorative plaques and display windows lining the halls.

Doorways are inset in marble and often are adorned with gold leaf terra cotta tile work.

Even the water fountains are an impressive art deco design.

LIBRARY

Entering the library through the gold leaf topped doors introduces a totally different motif than the hallway. The library is more serene using pastel blue and green wood with painted gold trim.

The room has ample natural light showing through a wall of windows. Additional lighting is provided by different designs of art deco lights than the hallway.

EAST AND WEST VESTIBULES

The vestibules for the east and west doors are essentially identical. Exterior deco green doors open to tomato red terra cotta tile walls. The ceiling molding is an art deco triangle design.

On each side of the entryway are decorative brass heating vents. The glass inner doors are a matching deco design to the exterior doors. Above the inner doorway is a tile with gold leaf trimming.

Will Rogers High School has one of the most attractive auditoriums of any school. It is lit by two distinctly different sets of art deco lights. One set lights the balcony where the other lights beneath it.

The style and color of the molding is the same red and gold leaf that is used in the school hallways.

In front of the stage is a 1903 museum quality Wurlitzer pipe organ that is currently in funding stage for restoration.

Decorative air vents and organ chamber space loom over door mantles above the stage doors to the auditorium. Hanging to each side of these doors are twenty foot tall light sconces.

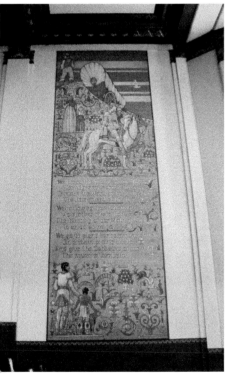

The most striking feature of the auditorium is the 32 by 10 foot mural. The artistic elements of the auditorium, including the mural, were designed and painted by Chicago artist, Alex C. Rindskoph.

In the center of the mural are three stanzas from the poem,

"The Kansas Immigrants"

by John Greenleaf Whittier

We cross the prairies as of old
The pilgrims crossed the sea
To make the West as they the East
The Homestead of the free.

We're flowing from our native hills.
As our free rivers flow:
The blessing of our Mother-land
Is on us as we go.

We go to plant her common schools
On distant prairie swells,
And give the Sabbaths of the wild
The music of her bells.

The Gillette-Tyrrell Building (often referred to as the Pythian) was originally designed to have thirteen floors but due to budget limitations was reduced to three floors.

The building is one of Tulsa's most impressive Art Deco examples with a unique décor both inside and outside. Strong vertical zigzag motifs are expressed on the exterior walls of the building. Edward Saunders, the building architect, described the building as integrating several styles of architecture including Italian, Spanish, and American Indian motifs.

EXTERIOR DESIGN

Built: 1930
Deco Style: Zigzag
Designed By: Edward W. Saunders
NRIS: 82003703
Address: 423 S. Boulder

The building still has the original richly decorated tiled interior and terra cotta exterior which are testaments to the craftsmanship and durability of the materials.

The exterior is covered by eye catching terra-cotta in a Zigzag vertical design. The blue and gold parapet along the roofline is striking.

Interior Designs

North-South Hall
The Gillette Terrell building has a richly decorated lobby with colorful tile walls and mosaic tile floors.

Tiled Walls
The tiled half walls are sectioned by vertical zigzag patterns topped by individually unique mosaics.

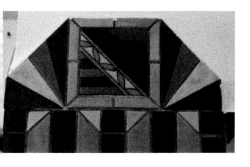

TILE FLOORS
The tile floor exhibits a unique American Indian zigzag deco style.

MOLDED SUSPENDED CEILINGS

The ceilings are ornately molded coffered plaster. Complex geometric art deco designs adorn beams and molding around the ceiling sections.

The variety of styles seen in the shells are reminiscent of the Spanish styles. It is a unique combination with Italian flowers and various Native American symbols.

Lighting is provided by etched glass windows above each doorway and art deco glass lanterns suspended from the center of the ceiling modules.

STAIRWELL & MEZZANINE

The North-South and East-West hallways intersect a lobby with elevators and an open mezzanine balcony.

A stairwell with cast iron railings and tile steps leads to the balcony. Light fixtures are inset and centered in a deco pattern radiating from the light.

EXTERIOR DESIGNS

Bishop Francis Kelly, for whom Bishop Kelly High School is named, brought Francis Byrne from Chicago to design a church that was "something both modern and authentic to Catholic worship". Byrne, who had worked for Frank Lloyd Wright in Chicago, utilized a Zigzag design incorporating Gothic and Byzantine features. The design was so innovative and radical ,compared to typical churches, that many Catholics were outraged by the design.

Built:	1929
Deco Style:	Zigzag
Designed By:	Francis Barry Byrne
	Bruce Goff
Artist:	Alphonso Ainnelli
Address	423 S. Boulder

Alfonso Iannelli was hired as the primary art designer and was responsible for the terra-cotta ornamentation including the spires around the exterior of the building and design of the stained glass windows. The design of the sanctuary is essentially square with strong vertical influences, crowned by a ceiling of dark polished wood slats. The two mosaics over the side altars were designed by Tulsa architect, Bruce Goff. When the church was dedicated in 1928, it was the first church in the world to be dedicated as "Christ the King".

The CHRIST THE KING mosaic, designed by Emil Frei, displays a rich Byzantine influence. Jesus is represented wearing the robes of a Byzantine emperor. His kingly stature is symbolized by the crown, scepter and orb which he caries.

The ORGAN PIPES over the west side of the sanctuary are patterned to represent the shape of a crown.

The TERRAZZO FLOOR design in front of the altar displays brown lines that spread to the communion rail and out into the church congregation from an eight pointed star, representative of the presence of Christ. The design represents John 15:5 "I am the vine and you are the branches."

Fourteen "STATIONS OF THE CROSS" are represented in white marble sculptures inset in the sanctuary walls.

EIGHT POINTED STARS are found through out the church. The design represents an eighth day of creation when God created Christ.

All religious information for this section comes from "Upon This Rock I Will Build My Church", a publication of Christ the King Church.

Italian artist, Alphonso Iannelli, designed the stained glass windows and interior art work of the church. The stained glass windows in the sanctuary depict five Saints and five Kings of the Christian era. The kings are all carrying their crowns in respect to Christ who is wearing his crown in the mosaic over the altar.

On the left is Saint Louis of France, who became King at the age of 22 in 1236. Next is Saint Edward, the confessor of England, who founded Westminster Abby and was the last Anglo Saxon King of England. In the center is Saint Stephen, considered the founder of Hungary. To his right is Saint Henry II of Bavaria and Saint Wenceslas who established Christianity in Czechoslovakia.

SOUTH STAINED GLASS WINDOWS

The south windows display, from west to east, depictions of King Melchizedek, King David and the three Magi. Abraham came before Melchizedek and in exchange for 10% of his property and earnings the king provided Abraham protection and his blessing. That became the basis for tithing in the church. King David united the Jewish tribes into a unified nation.

6. UNION DEPOT

The Tulsa Union Depot was a passenger railway station that served as Tulsa's train station from 1931 to 1967. It was built by the U. S. Public Works Administration in an Art-Deco style. It was called "Union Station because it unified the smaller Frisco, Katy, and Santa Fe train depots in Tulsa.

EXTERIOR DESIGNS

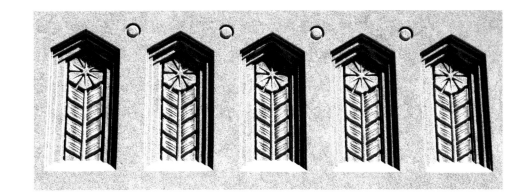

The exterior of the building is a Bedford stone with a rugged utilitarian appearance. Machinery is a theme expressed through the art deco building design. Most of the building decorations are over windows and along a parapet encircling the building. At the front and back of the building are two tower like structures giving the building a castle like facade.

Built:	1931
Deco Style:	PWA
Designed By:	R. C. Stephens
Address:	3 S. Boston Avenue

The north side of the building is adjacent to the railroad tracks and has the stairways that led to the passenger loading ramps. After deteriorating for years, the building was restored in the 1980's and converted into office space. In 2007, the Depot became the home of the Oklahoma Jazz Hall of Fame and is called the "Jazz Depot". The building interior has been modernized which has eliminated the high vaulted ceilings in the lobby, although the arched windows and doorways were retained.

Built:	1928
Deco Style:	Zigzag
Designed By	Arthur Atkinson
	Frederick Kershner
NRIS:	84003458
Address:	624 S. Boston Avenue

EXTERIOR DESIGNS

Tulsa had great financial growth in the late 1920's. This led Oklahoma Natural Gas to move its offices from Oklahoma City to Tulsa. They chose to build a ten story Art Deco structure that set a benchmark for future Art Deco buildings in Tulsa.

Notice the four piers that run the entire length of the of the building vertically, giving it a strong art deco zigzag style features.

The south portico shelters the main entrance to the building and features an art deco styled "ONG" (Oklahoma Natural Gas) over the door.

The first two floors and mezzanine are covered with a decorative façade that contrasts in color with the brick on the rest of the building.

Interior Designs

The interior design and materials are lavish. Oklahoma Natural Gas spent more than utility companies normally spend on public buildings to promote their success and impress Tulsa business people.

The foyer in the building is quite small but very decorative. It has ornate marble elevator door frames and assorted brass accessories in the lobby.

To the east of the foyer is a large lobby that has been converted into a ballroom for events. It is kept locked, but can be viewed by taking the elevator to the mezzanine.

8. FIRE ALARM BUILDING

The Fire Alarm building was built to centralize the fire alarm systems for all of Tulsa. Alarms came into this building and operators dispatched firemen from various parts of the city as needed. This octagonal building features terra cotta frieze work depicting a Mayan culture theme with double-headed dragons connected to stylized hoses. The exterior of the building has a great deal of terra cotta decoration. The building was used by the fire department until 1984 and is currently the headquarters of the American Lung Association of Oklahoma.

Built: 1930
Deco Style: PWA
Designed By: Frederick V. Kershner
NRIS: 03000879
Address   1010 E. 8th Street

EXTERIOR DESIGNS

The terra cotta panel above the front door features a male figure with alarm communications tape running through his hands. To either side are helmeted firefighters. Below him are two dragons with fire hoses making up their heads. The lightning bolts are intended to suggest speed and energy. The front façade uses a reoccurring theme of a double-headed dragons which are common in Mayan culture and refer to the gathering of energy from the earth.

At the rear of the building are four gargoyle-like sculptures topped with a hatchet.

69

Built in 1932, the Fair Grounds Pavilion is a PWA styled building. The exterior of the building is extraordinarily decorative with gold brick and color coordinated terra cotta ornamentation.

It is unusual for a building built in this time period to be so ornamental. Notice in the picture to the right how a ram head is used to embellish a building corner.

Built: 1932
Deco Style: PWA
Designed By: Leland I. Shumway
Artist:
Address: Expo Square 21st & Jamestown

Each of eight building entrances has a decorative portico covered by multi-colored terra cotta panels depicting horse, cattle and ram heads organized in various ways.

10. WAREHOUSE / FARMERS MARKET

The old Farmers market is a one-story building with a unique terra cotta adorned tower. The "Farmers Market" was built in 1929 next to the railroad tracks and served as a major groceries provider until the Great Depression.   It later became Club Lido and hosted famous musicians like Cab Calloway and Duke Ellington.

Built:	1929
Deco Style:	Zigzag
Designed By:	B. Gaylord Noftsger
Artist:	
Address:	925 S. Elgin Avenue

The building retains an entrance to a small foyer covered by a decorative tower. On each side of the doors are red medallions on blue backgrounds.   One is representative of the progress of industry and displays a god holding an oil derrick and train engine. The other honors agriculture with a goddess holding a sheaf of wheat and a cornucopia.

Above the doorway is a stunning green and gold plaque topped with a gold brick tower with vertical pilaster emphasizing a strong Art Deco zigzag style. The tower pinnacle is a geometric design implemented with colorful tile insets, cutaways and terra cotta plaques.

RIVERSIDE STUDIO

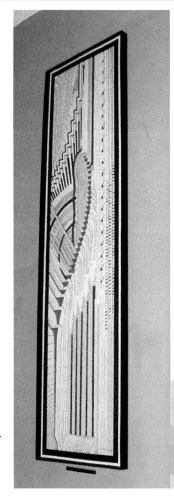

This structure was designed by architect, Bruce Goff for Mrs. Patti Adams Shriner. She was a music teacher and wanted a music studio with attached living quarters. The two-story stucco building sits on a sloping site facing the Arkansas River.

The building design was influenced by both Art Deco and International architectural styles. The inspiration for the design was a concept by Goff that he called "frozen music." This includes windows that resemble the punched tabs on a player piano paper tape, a circular window that resembles a sheet of music and an entry stairway that once resembled a piano keyboard.

Today it is a theater hosting the dramatic performance of an old fashioned melodrama, "The Drunkard."

Built:	1929
Deco Style:	Zigzag
Designed By:	Bruce Goff
NRIS:	01000656
Address:	1381 S. Riverside Drive

RICHARD LLOYD JONES RESIDENCE (WESTHOPE)

Westhope was the residence of Richard Lloyd Jones, the former owner of the "Tribune", one of Tulsa's major newspapers. The house was built by his cousin, famous architect, Frank Lloyd Wright. The house is a block design with concrete vertical pillars. Notice the vertically stacked windows between the columns that produce what Wright calls a transparent screen. The house incorporates carved exterior blocks with a decorative design unique to Westhope. This was a common Frank Lloyd Wright feature that serves as a distinct trademark for each structure he built.

Considering the house was built in 1929, it is extraordinarily modern. It is very spatial and had a chilled water system for cooling. It has an open floor plan that traverses over multiple plateaus. A Mayan pattern is used through the interior and exterior of the house. The flat roof of tar covered by pitch stones, was a new building innovation first introduced with this home.

Built: 1929
Deco Style: Zigzag
Designed By: Frank Lloyd Wright
NRIS: 75001575
Address: 3704 S. Birmingham Ave.

DANIEL WEBSTER HIGH SCHOOL

Daniel Webster High School opened in 1938 and was built using Work Progress Administration (WPA) funds. Artisans were employed to create a buff brick Art Deco structure. It has a very impressive entrance flanked with large rectangular columns. Two large metal torch lanterns flank the front entrance with the school name and a large clock hanging above. The aluminum plaques above the doors are of a classic Greek motif.

Built:	1938
Deco Style:	PWA
Designed By:	Arthur Atkinson
	John Duncan Forsyth
	Raymond Kerr
	William H. Wolaver
NRIS:	01000656
Address:	1919 W. 40th

OTHER SIGNIFICANT ART DECO

ADAH ROBINSON HOME

Built: 1927 & 1929
Deco Style: Zigzag
Designed By: Bruce Goff
              Joseph Koberling
Artist: Adah Robinson
Address: 1119 S. Owasso

Adah Robinson was a significant figure in the development of Art Deco in Tulsa. She was a high school art teacher who employed a former student, Bruce Goff, to design her home. Goff was an architectural child prodigy that began working as young as 13 on engineering construction projects for the engineering firm of Rush, Endicott and Rush. He admired Frank Lloyd Wright and emulated many of his features in the Robinson residence like a sunken fireplace and built-in angular furniture. Later Adah Robinson would hire Goff to collaborate on the design and architecture of the Boston Avenue Methodist Church.

BANK OF OKLAHOMA

Built: 1956
Deco Style: Streamline
Address: 31st & Harvard

BOULDER ON THE PARK

Wealthy Tulsan's Waite Phillips, W.G. Skelly and George S. Bole personally financed the building of Holland Hall School. The school moved in 1938 to a location around 28th and College. In 1947 the building was acquired by KTUL Radio who remodeled the building in the Art Deco Streamline Style. The building served as their broadcast studio. It was adorned with a neon KTUL sign. They referred to the building on the radio as "Boulder on the Park". They quit broadcasting from that location in 1955.

Built: 1923
Deco Style: Streamline
Designed By: Charles A. & Roy Wesley Sanderson
NRIS: 03000872
Address: 850 South Boulder Avenue

BROOK THEATER

Built: 1949
Deco Style: Streamline
Designed By:
Artist:
Address: 3401 S. Peoria Avenue

DAY-NITE CLEANERS

Built: 1946
Deco Style: Streamline
Designed By: William H. Wolaver
Address: 1012 South Elgin Ave.

KVOO STUDIOS

Built: 1956
Deco Style: Streamline
Designed By:
Artist:
Address: 3701 S. Peoria Avenue

CITY VETERINARY

Built: 1942
Deco Style: Streamline
Designed By: Joseph R. Koberling
NRIS: 08000848
Address: 3550 S. Peoria Avenue

SERVICE PIPELINE

Built: 1949
Deco Style: PWA
Designed By: Leon B. Senter
Address: 520 S. Cincinnati Ave.

TULSA MONUMENT CO.

Built: 1936
Deco Style: Streamline
Designed By: Harry H. Mahler
NRIS: 08000849
Address   1535 E. 11th Street

PHOENIX CLEANERS

Built: 1947
Deco Style: Streamline
Designed By:

Address: 125 E. 18th Street

PUBLIC SERVICE COMPANY

Built: 1929
Deco Style: Zigzag
Designed By: Arthur Atkinson
                Joseph Koberling
NRIS: 84003443
Address: 600 S. Main Street

Tulsa Art Deco Experience

Tulsa is one of the top Art Deco travel destinations in the world. Discover Tulsa's deco through over 200 stunning photographs and interesting commentary. This book displays all the significant Art Deco locations organized into five drivable tours.

$19.99

Tulsa Experience

Tulsa is a city of great history, tradition and beauty. Explore this unique city through over 400 photographs and notes of interest. Tulsa has world class museums, Route 66 and some of the country's best examples of Art Deco architecture. Experience one of America's most beautiful cities.

$15.99

Route 66 Tulsa - Where 66 intersects Art Deco

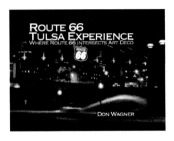

Route 66 is a 2400 mile long museum without walls. This book explores the section through Tulsa, OK. Nowhere on 66 is there more Art Deco than Tulsa. All routes through Tulsa and other prominent attractions and historical features are presented.

$15.99

Oklahoma City Experience

Oklahoma City is a vibrant growing metropolis with a rich history and promising future. This book visually explores the numerous attractions and development districts that make up this community including Bricktown, the Asian District, the Paseo, the Film Exchange District, Stockyard City, Automobile Alley, the Oklahoma River and much more.

$19.99

Route 66 Oklahoma Experience

Oklahoma has more miles of Route 66 than any other state. Learn about the Sidewalk Highway, Round Barn, Blue Whale and other fascinating attractions. Visually discover the Mother Road in Oklahoma with this exciting and informative book.

$15.99

OKLAHOMA TOURIST GUIDES

Oklahoma Tourist Guides Inc.
www.Tulsa-Books.com
(918) 693-1198
DON.WAGNER.OK@GMAIL.COM